Tides of Change

Contents

Features

Why were camels a popular form of transport for ancient Chinese traders? Turn to page 16 for more details.

How do you design something as large as a city? See **A Planned City** on page 22 to find out about a city designed in 1913.

Do you know some computers can be programmed to behave like people? See **What Is Artificial Intelligence?** on page 25.

Do you think technology should continue to change and advance as rapidly as possible? Check out **Turning the Tide** on page 28.

What is an "aging population"?
Visit www.rigbyinfoquest.com
for more about POPULATION.

Centuries of Change

The world has changed so much over the last 150 years that it could perhaps be unrecognizable to people who lived in the nineteenth and early twentieth centuries. There have been many changes to the landscape caused by erupting volcanoes, earthquakes, erosion, and weathering. However, human discoveries, inventions, and population growth have brought about the most significant changes.

Technological advances in science, transportation, communication, and medicine have been enormous. Transportation has changed dramatically, and today many people are able to travel widely throughout their own country and around the world. Communications technology has advanced so that people in different parts of the world can communicate instantly with each other by using a telephone or a computer. Medical discoveries have meant that people's **life expectancies** have increased in many parts of the world.

In the early 1900s, people calling long distance, or even over short distances in some areas, had to speak to a telephone operator before they could be connected.

Although many urban centers use high-tech equipment for almost everything from transportation to communications, many rural areas in the world have remained unchanged for hundreds of years.

Changes to the Land

Earth is always moving, and the landscape is always changing. Earthquakes and erupting volcanoes can cause sudden, often destructive, changes to an area. Natural disasters such as floods, tornadoes, and droughts can also cause dramatic changes to the land. Sometimes people are forced to move and resettle in new areas.

Tornado

Changes to the land also take place slowly over thousands of years. Weathering and erosion, especially by waves and wind, can eat away at coastlines and cliffs. The places where houses stood hundreds of years ago may not exist today because of these natural processes.

People make changes to the land, too. In some areas, land has been **reclaimed** or rock has been blasted away to make room for housing and industry.

Polder

In some countries such as the Netherlands, people have been reclaiming land for many centuries. Areas in the Netherlands where the water has been drained are called polders. The polders region makes up two-fifths of the nation's landmass and contains some of the country's largest cities and most fertile farmland.

A Growing Population

Where in the World Do People Live?

Between 1950 and 2003, Earth's population increased from about 2.5 billion people to just over 6.3 billion. It is predicted that by the year 2050, there will be more than 9 billion people on Earth.

Some countries are densely populated. This means there is a large number of people living in a small area. Others are sparsely populated, with a small number of people living in a large area. Variations in weather and landscape are just two of the reasons for these population differences. For example, flat, fertile land is more densely populated than mountainous, dry land because it is easier for people to settle on and farm.

Key

Developed countries

Developing countries

Most densely populated areas

Population Spread

As countries develop, people are attracted to job opportunities in large cities. Urban areas have dense populations compared to rural areas.

Developed countries have 20% of the world's population, hold 80% of the world's wealth, and use 70% of the world's energy.

Developing countries have 80% of the world's population, hold 20% of the world's wealth, and use 30% of the world's energy.

SITESEEING
• PEOPLE & PLACES •

What is an "aging population"?

Visit www.rigbyinfoquest.com
for more about POPULATION.

Why Are There More People?

There are many reasons why the human population is increasing at a rapid rate. One of the most significant is that many people now have higher life expectancies than they did in the past. In developed parts of the world, medicines have improved so much that few people die of illnesses such as measles and influenza. There are cures for these illnesses and prevention in the form of vaccinations. Hygiene and living standards have also improved greatly, especially over the last 100 years. People have discovered that cleanliness is important for stopping the spread of germs.

Key

Less developed regions

More developed regions

Less developed regions: Africa, Latin America and the Caribbean, Asia (excluding Japan), Melanesia, Micronesia, Polynesia.

More developed regions: North America, Japan, Europe, Australia, New Zealand.

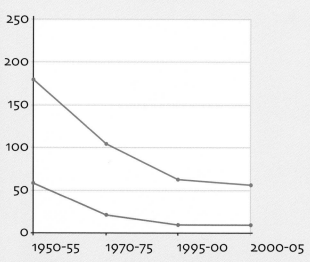

Infant Mortality Rates

The infant mortality rate measures how many infants die before reaching 12 months of age. The rate tells how many babies die each year for every 1,000 babies born. The measurement is an indication of the well-being of a nation.

Improved medical technology and surgical advances mean that people can often recover from accidents and injuries they may not have survived in the past. Cures for many diseases have been found. People have also become increasingly aware of the importance of exercise and a good diet for the prevention of some illnesses.

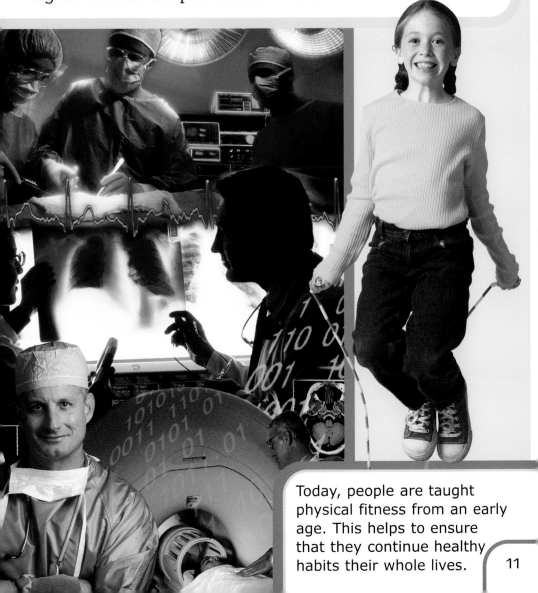

Today, people are taught physical fitness from an early age. This helps to ensure that they continue healthy habits their whole lives.

11

Sharing Resources

One of the world's most important resources is food. Food supply is largely dependent on farmers who grow crops and raise livestock. It is essential that food supply keeps up with the increase in the world's population. In some regions of the world, food production is increasing at a greater rate than the population, but food production falls short of population growth in other regions. It is important for governments to keep track of both population growth and food production to avoid food shortages.

Food supply varies from country to country and from year to year. A shortage of food can be caused by weather conditions such as droughts or floods. These and other causes mean that not all countries are able to produce all the food they need. Sometimes wealthy developed nations give aid, such as food and medical supplies, to developing countries.

Measuring Food Supply

A country's food supply depends not only on the amount of food produced but also on the number of people to feed. It is measured by how much food would be available to each person if the food was distributed evenly amongst the population.

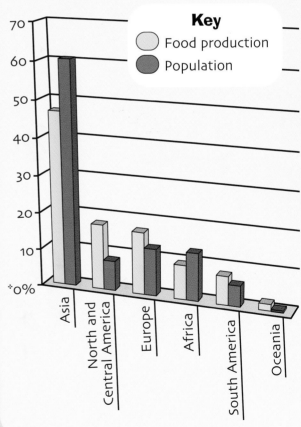

Key
- Food production
- Population

*Percent of world total

Moving Around the World

What Is Trade?

Buying and selling goods is called trade. People trade because they need or want things that other people can produce. People trade with each other in local markets. There is trade within a country, which is called domestic trade, and trade between countries, which is called international trade.

Some countries specialize in producing particular goods because they have the necessary resources. For example, Australia specializes in exporting beef because it has plenty of land on which to raise cattle. It exports to Japan and other countries where there is little space for this kind of farming. Japan specializes in industrial and electronic products, which it then exports to Australia and other countries. The United States, Germany, and Japan are the three largest importers and exporters in the world.

Changes Over Time in Trading Transportation

Camel   Sailing ship   Train

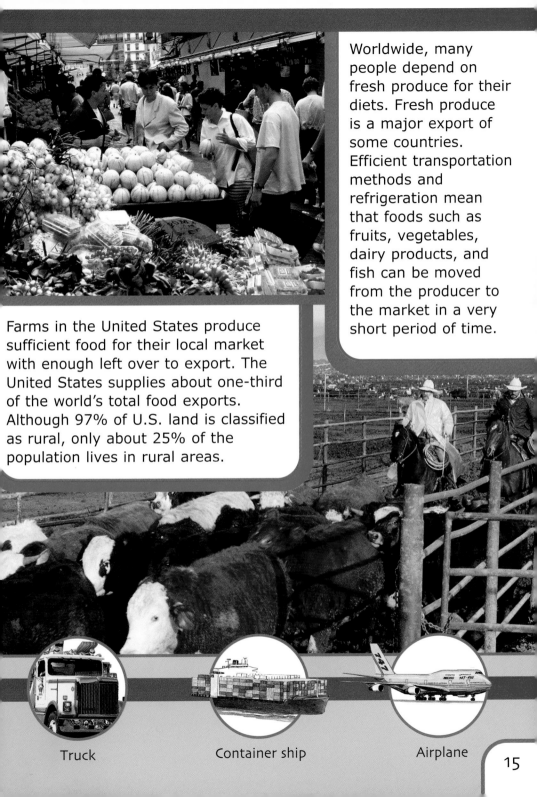

Worldwide, many people depend on fresh produce for their diets. Fresh produce is a major export of some countries. Efficient transportation methods and refrigeration mean that foods such as fruits, vegetables, dairy products, and fish can be moved from the producer to the market in a very short period of time.

Farms in the United States produce sufficient food for their local market with enough left over to export. The United States supplies about one-third of the world's total food exports. Although 97% of U.S. land is classified as rural, only about 25% of the population lives in rural areas.

Truck

Container ship

Airplane

Transporting Goods

Long ago, people traded with nearby villages. They could only trade as much as they could carry. When people began to use camels and other animals to carry goods, trading routes developed between towns. People living near waterways then invented sailboats so traders were able to travel to other countries by sea. However, sailors had poor navigational skills then, and many ships sank. By the 1400s, navigational skills and the design of ships had improved greatly and trade grew quickly.

Transportation has changed rapidly since the 1800s when the first engine-powered vehicles were invented. Today, trucks, trains, ships, and airplanes carry goods quickly and efficiently across countries and around the world. Traveling times are now so short that fresh goods such as flowers and fruit can be transported from one side of the world to the other.

TIME LINK

The ancient Chinese used camels to carry silk for trade with neighboring people in Central Asia. Camels were an excellent form of transportation because each camel could carry up to 440 pounds of cargo. They were also able to smell underground water supplies and protect their riders from sandstorms by huddling together.

Transporting cargo in containers is a fast, cost-effective way of moving goods around the world. Once packed into a container, the goods are transported by ship, truck, train, or airplane. About 90% of the world's **general cargo** is transported in containers.

People Movers

Millions of people around the world use transportation to take them to work or school every day. They take a bus or train, or they drive in a car. Some people travel regularly by airplane in their own country or to other countries around the world, often as part of their jobs.

People also move around the world for many other reasons. They visit family, they take vacations, or they move permanently to a new country. Travel to other countries has become quicker and easier over the last 50 years, and more people than ever before are moving around the world and settling in new countries. When people move, they take the cultures and customs of their home country with them. This means that many countries today are, or are becoming, multicultural. Today, people have a greater opportunity to learn about the cultures of other countries.

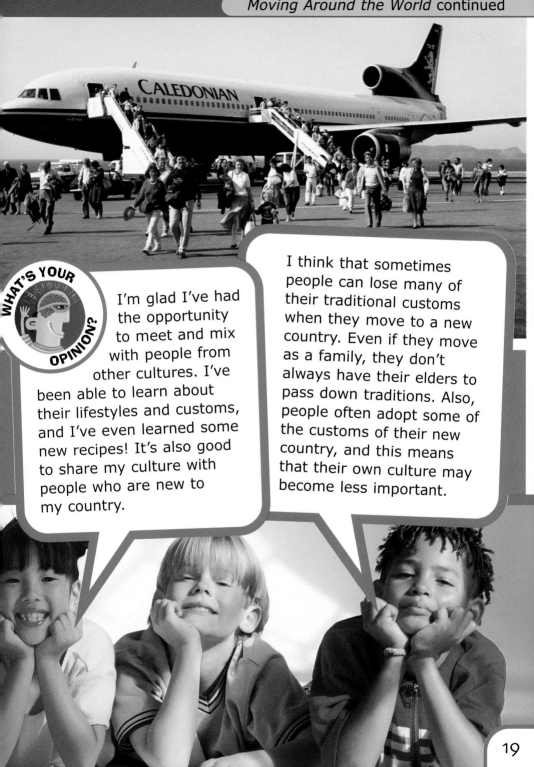

WHAT'S YOUR OPINION?

I'm glad I've had the opportunity to meet and mix with people from other cultures. I've been able to learn about their lifestyles and customs, and I've even learned some new recipes! It's also good to share my culture with people who are new to my country.

I think that sometimes people can lose many of their traditional customs when they move to a new country. Even if they move as a family, they don't always have their elders to pass down traditions. Also, people often adopt some of the customs of their new country, and this means that their own culture may become less important.

19

Using Energy

Traditionally, energy has been provided by animals, wind, and steam. The gasoline engine was invented at the end of the nineteenth century, and since then, millions of cars, ships, airplanes, trucks, and trains have been manufactured worldwide. Most of the energy to drive these vehicles comes from burning fossil fuels such as coal, oil, and natural gas.

Today, there are two main problems with using fossil fuels. Firstly, because there are so many vehicles driven daily throughout the world, people are worried about the air pollution that the release of substances such as carbon dioxide and smoke cause. Secondly, people are worried that the fossil fuels we are so dependent on will run out. The search is on for more uses of energy from **renewable resources.** Solar, hydroelectric, and geothermal energy are all renewable.

Although coal is still mined in many areas, there are fears that it will run out in the future because it is not a renewable resource.

Some Alternative Fuels

Nuclear power plants use uranium, a metal found in rock, to produce energy. Nuclear energy already accounts for about 17% of the world's electricity. However, many people are concerned about the safety of using nuclear energy, especially because there have been accidents at nuclear power plants that have caused widespread damage.

Solar energy uses sunlight to produce heat and power. It was used as long ago as 1882 when a French engineer invented a solar printing press. It is, however, more expensive than fossil fuels.

Hydroelectric power plants convert energy from falling water into electrical energy. About 20% of the world's electricity is produced this way. Hydroelectric power is cheaper to produce than power from fossil fuels, and it doesn't cause pollution.

Geothermal power plants produce power by using steam from underground sources. This is not a widely used energy source.

21

A Planned City

Canberra

Most large cities in the world have grown in size because they're close to trading routes or areas where industry or business attracts people. Some cities, however, have been specially planned. One example is Canberra, the capital city of Australia. In 1908, the Australian government decided that the small farming region was a suitable site on which to build the country's capital city. Although European settlement had already begun in Sydney and Melbourne, neither of these cities wanted the other city to be the capital. An international competition for the design of Canberra was announced in 1912. It was won by an American architect, Walter Burley Griffin.

The building of Griffin's plan began in 1913. Establishing the city took a long time, and it wasn't until the 1950s that the population began to grow. Since then, it has grown from 40,000 to more than 300,000. Today, Canberra has spread well beyond the 1913 plan. The care people have taken to plant trees and protect rivers, forests, and reserves has made Canberra a successful example of urban development.

Walter Burley Griffin faced the largest challenge of his life when he designed the city of Canberra, and he felt free to design modern architecture that differed from styles of the past. The drawing of his plan, created by his skilled wife, was 8 feet wide and 30 feet long when it was entered into the competition!

Parliament Buildings in the city

Technology

The Digital Revolution

Like the Industrial Revolution, discoveries in digital technology have brought about worldwide changes. New technology continually changes the way people learn, work, travel, and go about their everyday lives. Today, computers internally control nearly everything from vehicles and medical equipment to household devices and heavy machinery.

People use computers to play games, to get news and weather reports, and to gather information. They use them in their jobs and in their schools. This has been true for only a few years.

As new electronic devices are invented, they are becoming smaller and thinner. Devices such as personal computers, televisions, radios, video cassette recorders, CD players, and DVD players are always being redesigned. More and more we are taught, informed, and entertained by complicated electronic machinery.

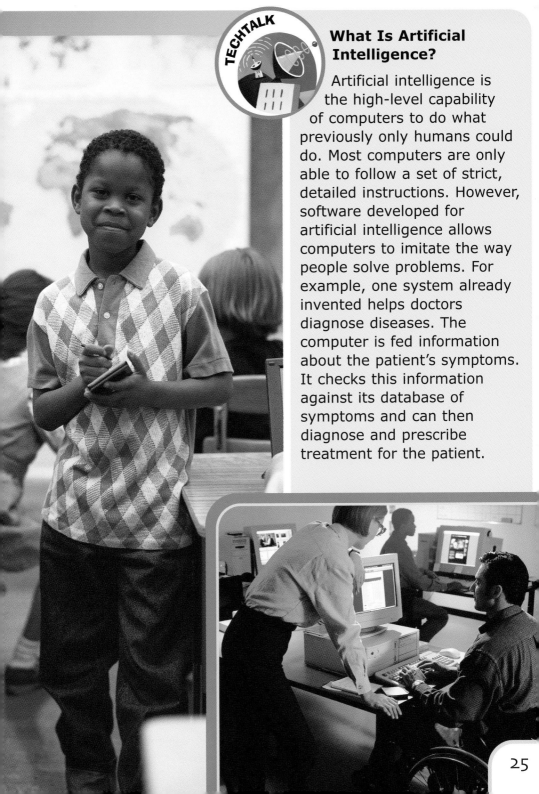

What Is Artificial Intelligence?

Artificial intelligence is the high-level capability of computers to do what previously only humans could do. Most computers are only able to follow a set of strict, detailed instructions. However, software developed for artificial intelligence allows computers to imitate the way people solve problems. For example, one system already invented helps doctors diagnose diseases. The computer is fed information about the patient's symptoms. It checks this information against its database of symptoms and can then diagnose and prescribe treatment for the patient.

Changing Careers

Long ago, many people were born into families who chose their children's careers. If you were the child of a farmer, a teacher, or a baker, for example, you would probably be expected to carry on the family tradition and do the same work. Today, however, jobs are more specialized, there are more choices for careers, and many people decide for themselves what they want to do.

Some jobs have changed very little over the centuries. For example, doctors in China thousands of years ago used acupuncture to ease pain and treat illnesses. Today, many doctors still use acupuncture, not only in China but also in many parts of the world. Other jobs have been invented only in the last few years as technology, transportation, communication, and medicine have changed and advanced.

Businesses such as bakeries were often run by families in the past.

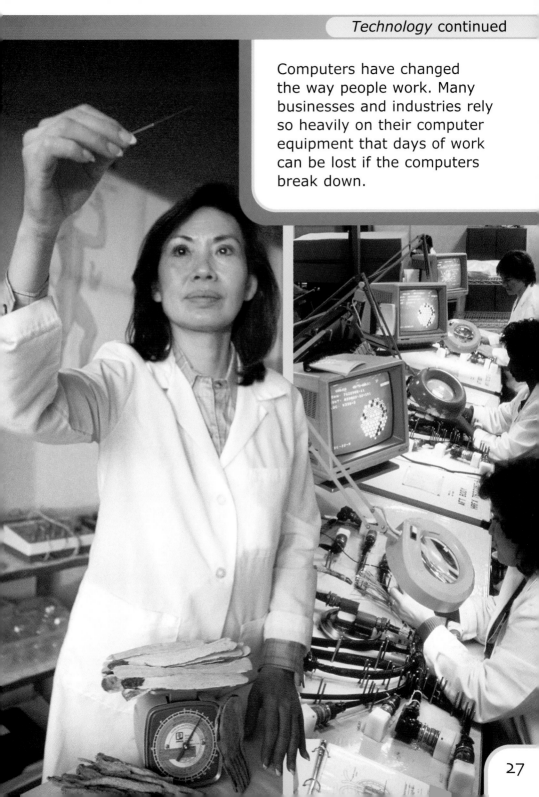

Computers have changed the way people work. Many businesses and industries rely so heavily on their computer equipment that days of work can be lost if the computers break down.

27

Turning the Tide

Sometimes, technological advances and changes in science, transportation, communication, and medicine have negative effects. For example, some "improved" vehicles have increased air pollution. Rapid development of computers means that current computers become **obsolete** in a very short time, and this creates **inorganic** waste.

Do you think we should continue making improvements to things such as computers and cars, or do you think we should stop now before we cause any more damage to ourselves and our planet?

Lion Yang, 11 years

I think we should keep improving cars until we can use electricity to power them all. If we use electricity, we won't need to use gas, and therefore we won't increase air pollution. I also think we need to make cars smaller so that there are fewer traffic jams in cities.

Louis Newton, 12 years

I think we should keep on making improvements in all areas of science and technology. We might discover something in the future that can correct the negative effects from earlier technologies. For example, waste eaters might be developed. We might be able to find a way of feeding homeless people in the future if we continue to develop genetically modified food. This food might grow faster and in larger quantities. I don't think we should stop progress in technology and science.

James Danaher, 12 years

I think that these kind of advances should have stopped years ago. We expect things to improve at such a fast rate that companies are always making new, sometimes unnecessary, products. We then throw out our old things, such as computers, and this causes pollution. Sometimes we do this just to get a bit more speed or a new computer game.

Lucretia Samson, 10 years

I think that we should stop and make do with what we've got. This will help stop pollution. We should, however, do more research on new technology that doesn't harm our environment.

Jaime Wilkinson, 12 years

We do need to keep on improving things, but we are going to have to draw the line somewhere. I think we should only continue developing in areas that are absolutely necessary.

Glossary

developed countries – countries that have a high level of industrialization and a high standard of living

developing countries – countries that have little industry and a low standard of living

general cargo – packaged goods. General cargo consists of products such as food, machinery, chemicals, shoes, and motor vehicles. There are special general cargo ships to carry packaged goods.

inorganic – made of matter other than plant or animal matter. Inorganic materials do not break down easily and must be disposed of carefully to avoid environmental damage.

life expectancy – the amount of time a person can expect to live based on the average life spans of similar people in similar conditions

obsolete – no longer used or useful. Technology advances so quickly that computers can sometimes become obsolete after only a few years.

reclaim – to make wasteland or land underwater suitable for human use by clearing and draining it

renewable resources – energy sources that are able to be used more than once because they are constantly available. Fossil fuels are not renewable, and this is why there is concern that our supply of them will someday run out.

Index

Bibliography

Challoner, Jack. *Energy.* Dorling Kindersley, 1993.

Hoare, Stephen. *20th Century Inventions, Digital Revolution.* Wayland Publishers Limited, 1998.

Jollands, David (Editor). *Machines, Power and Transport.* Cambridge University Press, 1984.

Oxland, Chris. *20th Century Inventions, Telecommunications.* Wayland Publishers Limited, 1996.

Parker, Steve. *Medicine.* Dorling Kindersley, 1995.

Research Starters

1 People have gone from traveling at speeds of only a few miles per hour to traveling faster than the speed of sound. Research some of the fastest current vehicle speeds. Do you think people will continue to invent machines that travel even faster? If so, what kind of machine can you imagine? Sketch your futuristic invention.

2 Choose a large city that interests you and research to figure out why it grew in that location. Draw a plan showing the location of the housing, the business areas, the industrial areas, and the parks and reserves. If you had been able to plan this city from the start, what would you have done differently?

3 Research to list several machines or items that have become obsolete and why. Then list currently used items in your home and school that you think might become obsolete in the future. How much longer do you think you will use them? What might replace them?

4 Interview a grandparent or older person in your community to find out what their generation does with appliances and other items that are no longer in good working order. Do they have the same attitude toward replacing items that your generation has?